How to use this book

There are 52 basic letter shapes in written English (**Aa**–**Zz**) and they are all abstract shapes

In Letterland these abstract shapes are linked to child-friendly characters that children love ~~quickly get to know.~~ When your child sees the Letterland characters linked to the letter shapes, the risk of confusing all these abstract shapes is greatly reduced. You'll then find that even when you show the plain black letter shape your child will 'see' the character in their mind's eye, helping them remember the sound and how to form the letter shape.

It's important for your child to learn the right 'movement pathway' for each letter. Correct formation ensures that the letters begin and end in the right place. This is especially important when your child moves on to the next stages of joined-up handwriting. If young children are allowed to form letters 'their own way' these habits quickly become established and can be very difficult to correct later.

Pages 17-26 focus on joining letter shapes together. Discover where the joins and breaks are, so letters can be formed in the most efficient way. Pages 27-31 feature high frequency words - words we use most in the English language. By practising these particular words the benefits should soon appear in virtually every piece of writing.

Letter shapes

The Letterland characters and the letter shapes to trace over are in the popular 'Sassoon' font. This pre-cursive font is used widely in schools. Please note that the letters 'k' and 'f' have two variant shapes. Choose whichever your child is most familiar with.

Rhymes

There is a rhyme to help children remember the correct letter formation. Read the rhyme to your child as they write. Also available as *Handwriting Songs* (to download or listen with *Phonics Online*). See **www.letterland.com** for further information.

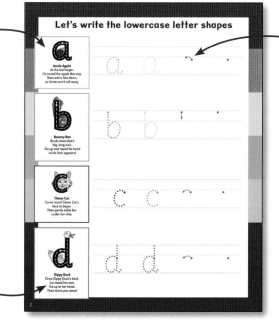

Handwriting practice

Dots and arrows to help with starting positions and correct letter formation. Letter shapes become more faint so children gradually learn to form letters on their own.

Wipe-clean

Each page is wipe-clean so your child can write over the letter shapes with the special pen over and over again.

Correct Handwriting Positions

Left-hander

Paper side edge

Table edge

Elbows off the table

Right-hander

Paper bottom edge

Table edge

Chair slightly tilted

Let's write the lowercase letter shapes

Annie Apple
At the leaf begin.
Go round the apple this way.
Then add a line down,
so Annie won't roll away.

Bouncy Ben
Brush down Ben's
big, long ears.
Go up and round his head
so his face appears!

Clever Cat
Curve round Clever Cat's
face to begin.
Then gently tickle her
under her chin.

Dippy Duck
Draw Dippy Duck's back.
Go round her tum.
Go up to her head.
Then down you come!

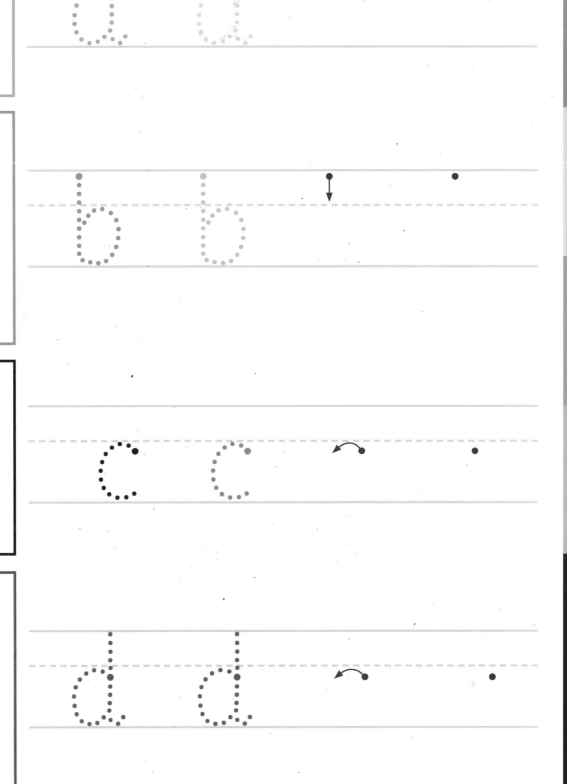

Eddy Elephant
Ed has a headband.
Draw it and then
stroke round his head
and his trunk to the end.

Firefighter Fred
First draw Fred's helmet.
Then go down a way.
Give him some arms
and he'll put out the blaze.

Alternate f
Sometimes the letter shape
looks more like this.

Golden Girl
Go round Golden Girl's head.
Go down her golden hair.
Then curve to make her swing,
so she can sit there.

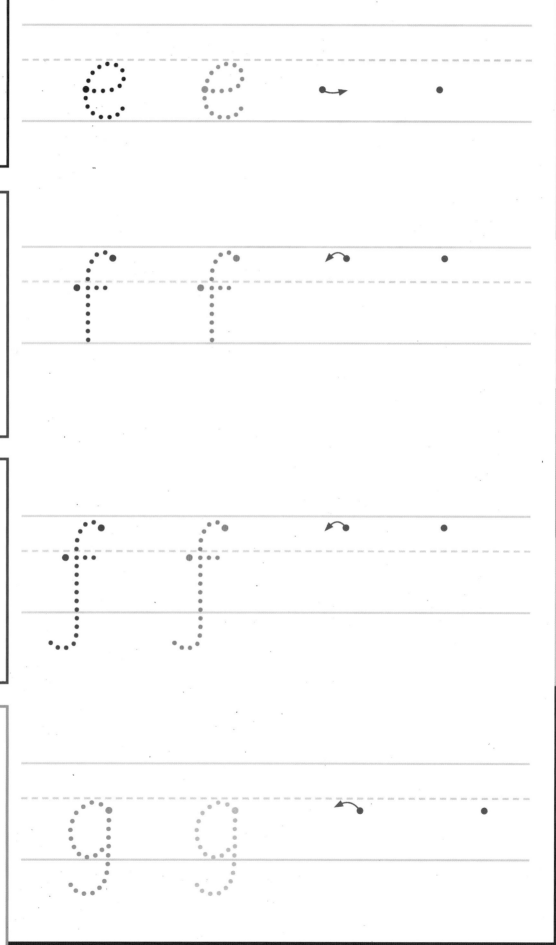

Harry Hat Man

Hurry from the Hat Man's head
down to his heel on the ground.
Go up and bend his knee over,
so he'll hop while
he makes his sound.

Impy Ink

Inside the ink bottle
draw a line.
Add an inky dot.
That's fine!

Jumping Jim

Just draw down Jim,
bending his knees.
Then add the one ball
which everyone sees.

Kicking King

Kicking King's body
is a straight stick.
Add his arm, then his leg,
so he can kick!

Alternate k
Sometimes the letter shape looks more like this.

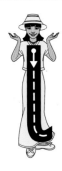

Lucy Lamp Light
Lucy looks like one long line.
Go straight from head to foot
and she's ready to shine!

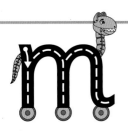

Munching Mike
Make Munching Mike's
back leg first,
then his second leg, and third,
so he can go munch-munching
in a word.

Noisy Nick
'Now bang my nail,'
Noisy Nick said.
'Go up and over
around my head.'

Oscar Orange
On Oscar Orange
start at the top.
Go all the way round him,
and... then stop.

Peter Puppy
Pat Peter Puppy properly.
First stroke down his ear,
then up and round his face
so he won't shed a tear.

Quarrelsome Queen
Quickly go round the
Queen's cross face.
Then comb her beautiful
hair into place.

Red Robot
Run down Red Robot's body.
Go up to his arm and his hand.
Then watch out for this robot
roaming round Letterland.

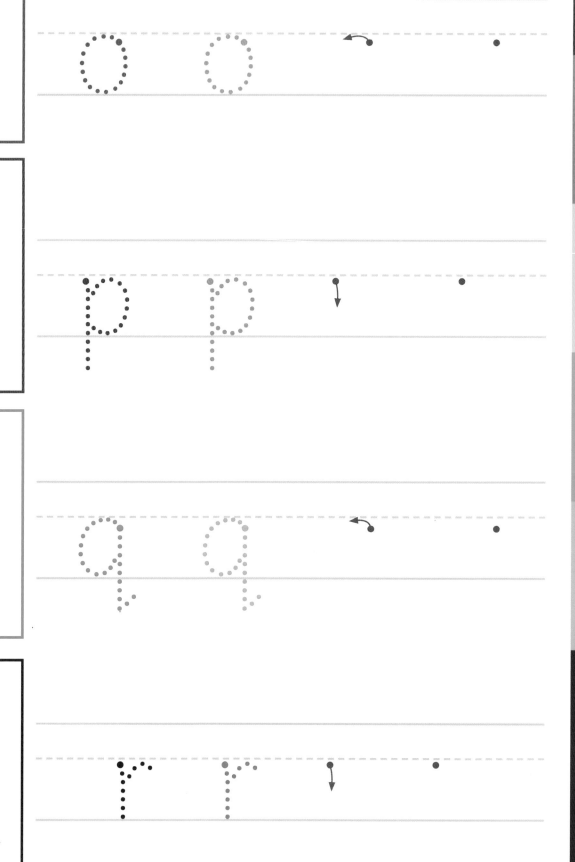

Sammy Snake
Start at Sam's head
where he can see.
Stroke down to his tail,
oh so care-ful-ly!

Talking Tess
Tall as a tower make
Talking Tess stand.
Go from head to toe,
and then from hand to hand.

Uppy Umbrella
Under the umbrella
draw a shape like a cup.
Then draw a straight line
so it won't tip up.

Vicky Violet
Very neatly,
start at the top.
Draw down your vase,
then up and stop.

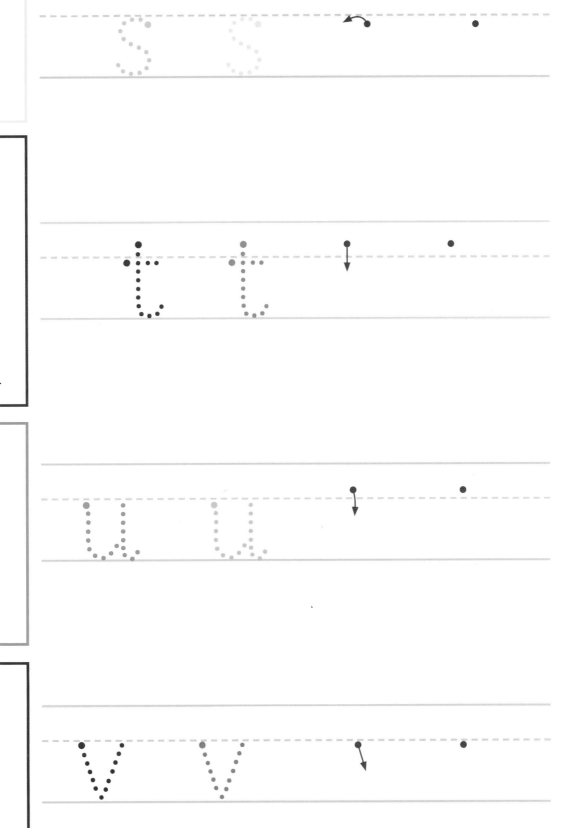

Walter Walrus
When you draw
the Walrus' wells,
with wild and wavy water,
whizz down and up and then...,
whizz down and up again.

Fix-it Max
Fix two sticks,
to look like this.
That's how to draw
a little kiss.

Yellow Yo-yo Man
You first make the yo-yo sack
on the Yo-yo Man's back,
and then go down to his toes
so he can sell his yo-yos.

Zig Zag Zebra
Zip along Zig Zag's nose.
Stroke her neck...,
stroke her back...
Zzzoom! Away she goes.

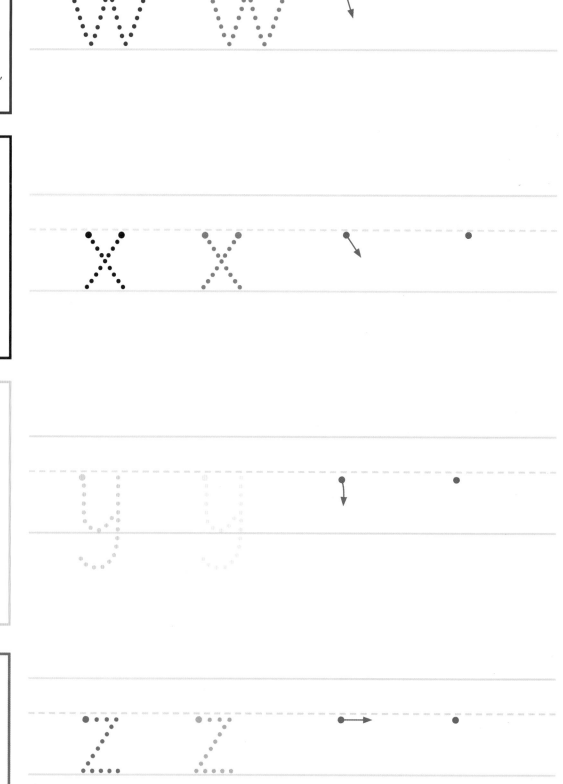

Let's write the uppercase letter shapes

Annie Apple's Applestand
At the applestand top
start down to the line.
And again from the top,
start the other way. Fine!
Then add a shelf for Annie to sit
with lots of space
for her friends to fit.

Bouncy Ben balances a ball
Brush down Bouncy Ben's
big brown ear,
Then go 'round his balancing ball,
Next brush gently 'round his head,
but take care that his ball won't fall.

Clever Cat gets bigger
Come, make a BIG curve
'round Clever Cat's face,
to show us her letter
when it's uppercase.

Dippy Duck's Duck Door
Draw down from the top of
Dippy Duck's door.
Go all the way down to the floor.
Then start at the top once more.
Curve down to the ground
for a funny-shaped door.

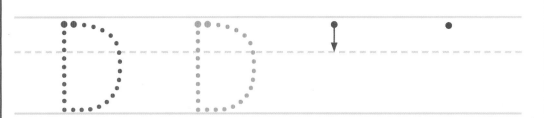

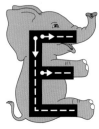

Eddy Elephant's on-End trick

Eddy Elephant loves sitting on end.
Draw down from his head
to his leg at the end.
Draw a line for his trunk,
and one leg in the air.
That's how to make Eddy
sitting right there!

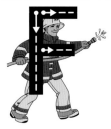

Firefighter Fred gets bigger

For uppercase Firefighter Fred,
go down to his feet from his head.
Go across at his helmet.
Then add his arm, so he'll use his
hose to keep us from harm.

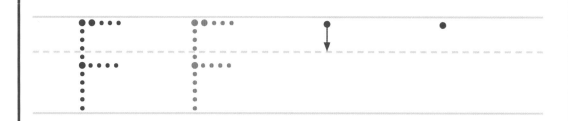

Golden Girl's Go-cart

Go 'round in nearly a circle
to draw Golden Girl's fast go-cart.
Go across with a short straight line,
so her go-cart is ready to start.

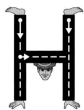

Harry Hat Man's Handstand

Hurry from heel to hand,
then again from heel to hand.
Then add a line across
for the Hat Man's big handstand!

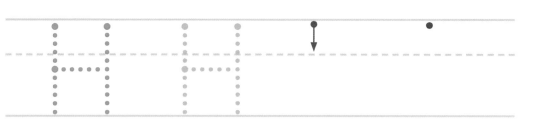

Impy Ink's Ink Pen
Impy Ink's pen is a long, thin line.
Add two stands if you like.
That's fine!

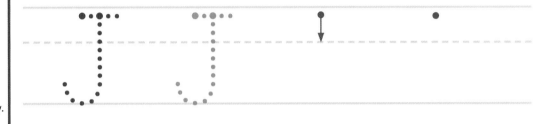

Jumping Jim jumps up
Jumping Jim can jump very high,
so we can't see his head up in the sky.
Go right down his body,
bending his knees.
For his arms add a line –
which everyone sees!

Kicking King gets bigger
Kicking King's body is a straight stick.
Make his arm and leg looooong
for a really big KICK!

Lucy Lamp Light gets longer
Lucy Lamp Light likes starting
important words.
That's when her legs grow quite long.
Go straight down her body.
Put her legs on the line.
Do that – and you cannot go wrong!

Munching Mike's Mum
Move from Mike's Mum's tail
drawing down to her back wheel.
At the top go down, up,
and down again,
so she can munch a big meal!
Mmmm!

Noisy Nick's New Nails
Noisy Nick's letter has
three big nails:
one..., and two... and three.
Go down 1, go down 2,
next up number 3
as quick as you can be!

Oscar Orange gets bigger
On Oscar Orange start at the top.
Go all the way 'round him.
Make him BIG... and then stop!

Peter Puppy pops up
Peter Puppy pops up
for important words.
From the back of his head
go down to the ground.
Then go right 'round his face
so he'll whisper his sound.

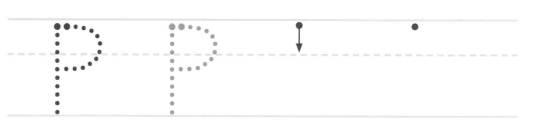

Quarrelsome Queen's Quiet Room
Quickly draw the Queen's Quiet Room.
Make it cosy and round.
Then add a place where she can sit
whenever she needs to calm down.

Red Robot changes shape
Ready? Draw Red Robot's back
and one leg that is straight.
Add a curve, and another leg,
so he's ready to roller skate!

Sammy Snake gets bigger
Start high on your page
where Sammy Snake can see.
Make his letter BIG,
oh, so care-ful-ly!

Talking Tess grows longer
Talking Tess can grow very tall.
With her head in the clouds
you can't see her at all.
So draw a straight line from
her neck to her feet,
then another, left-to-right,
for her arms, straight and neat.

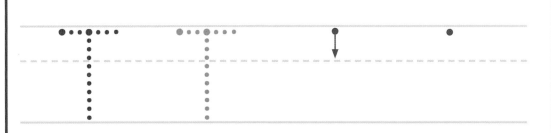

Uppy Umbrella gets bigger

Under Uppy Umbrella
draw a BIG shape like a cup.
Then draw a straight line
all the way down
so it won't tip up.

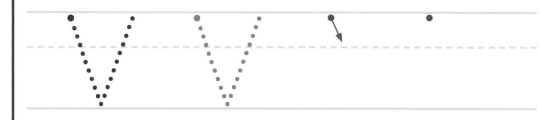

Vicky's Vase gets bigger

Vicky Violet has one
VERY BIG vase.
It's much bigger than her little one.
Start at the top,
slant down to the line.
Draw back up to the top,
and it's done!

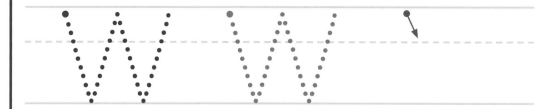

Walter Walrus gets bigger

When Walter Walrus wants BIG wells
he takes a deep breath and he swells!
So whizz down and up and then...
whizz down and up again!

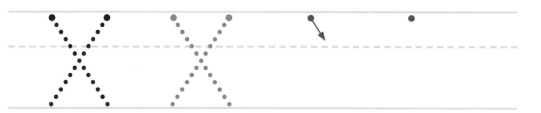

Fix-it Max gets bigger

Fix-it Max sends you a BIG kiss!
Cross two big sticks to look like this!

Yellow yo-yo Man steps up
Yes, start at the Yo-yo Man's sack.
Go down that sack at the back.
Then go down from his head
to his toes, so he'll stand on the line
to sell his yo-yos!

Zig Zag Zebra gets bigger
Zig Zag Zebra enjoys looking BIG,
so give her a LONG nose,
LONGER neck, and LONG back.
Zzzoom! Away she goes.

I know my letter shapes.
I can write my name.

My name is

Write your name on the line.

15

Aa-Zz Handwriting Practice

Let's trace all of the uppercase and lowercase letter shapes.

Reading Direction

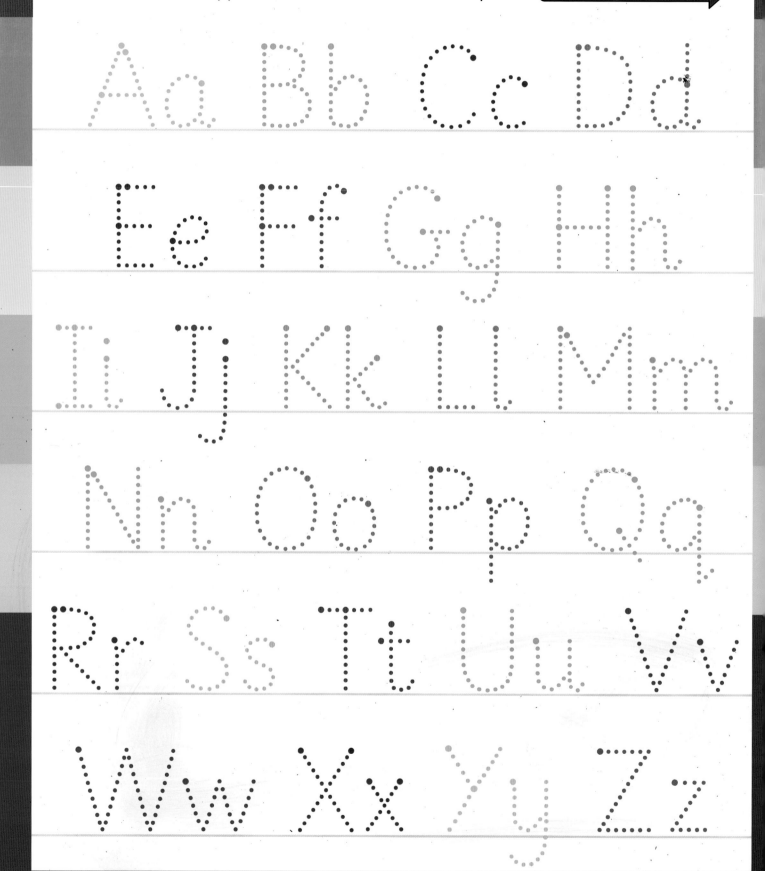

Small letters

Trace and write

 a   a   a

 c   c   c

 e   e   e

 i   i   i

 m   m   m

 n   n   n

 o   o   o

Small letters

Trace and write

 r   r   r   r   ·   ·

 s   s   s   s   ·   ·

 u   u   u   u   ·   ·

 v   v   v   v   ·   ·

 w   w   w   w   ·   ·

 x   x   x   x   ·   ·

 z   z   z   z   ·   ·

Tall letters

Trace and write

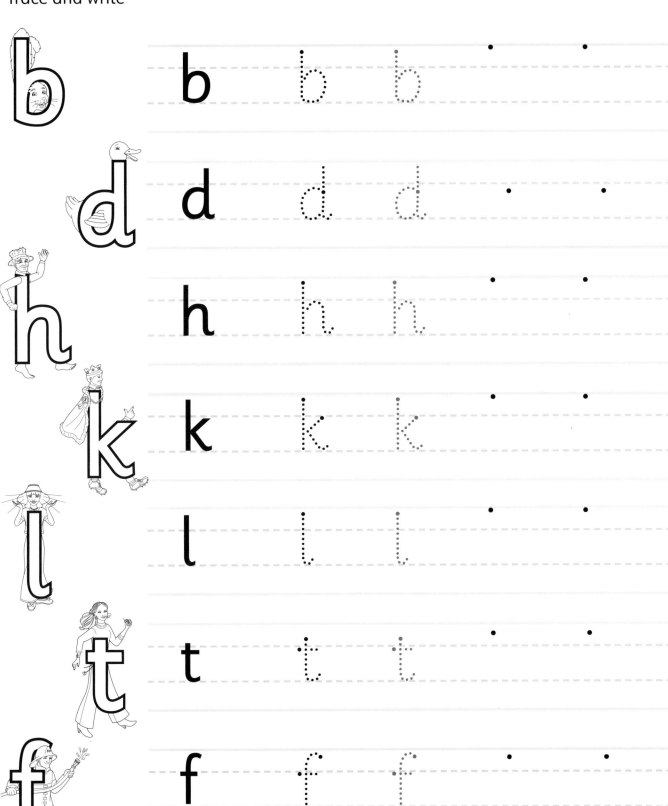

Descenders

Trace and write

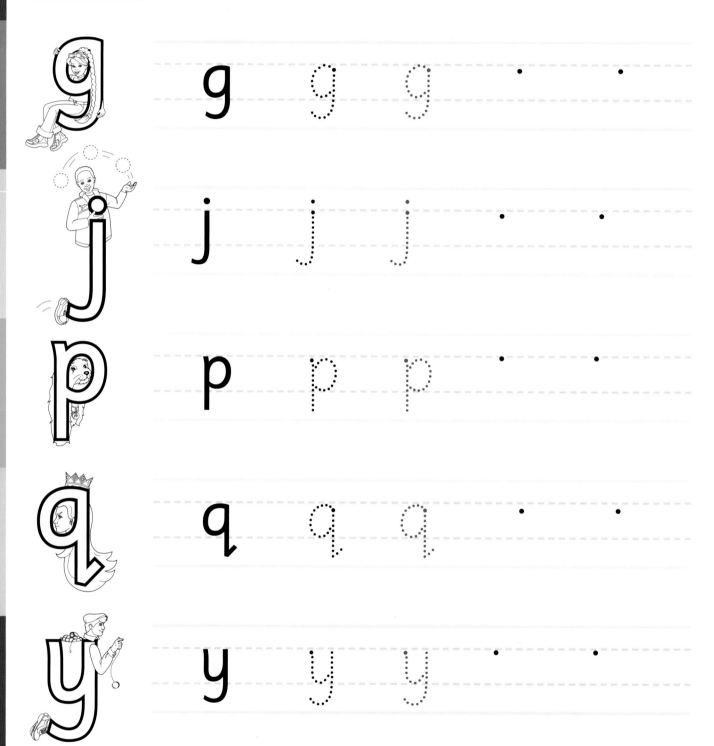

Join lines

Let's trace the join lines. **Break letters** - these letters often do not have an exit stroke and don't join on to other letters in a word: **b**, **g**, **j**, **p**, **q**, **x**, **y**, **z**.

mmm  nnnn

oooo  pppp

qu qu rrrr

sssss ttttt

uuuuu vvvv

www xxx

yyyy  zzzz

Joining letters together

Trace and write

jam

pen

bat

zip

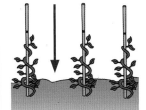

gap

Trace and write

cat

map

hand

nuts

10 *ten*

Trace and write

rat

frog

on

off

van

Trace and write

web

flag

doll

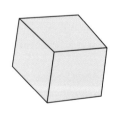
object

ring

High-frequency words

These are the 100 most commonly used words in the whole English language. Trace and then write them on the lines.

the		she
and		is
a		for
to		at
said		his
in		but
he		that
I		with
of		all
it		we
was		can
you		are
they		up
on		had

Trace and write

my	·	·	were	· ·
her	·	·	go	· ·
what	·	·	little	· ·
there	·	·	as	· ·
out	·	·	no	· ·
this	·	·	mum	· ·
have	·	·	one	· ·
went	·	·	them	· ·
be	·	·	do	· ·
like	·	·	me	· ·
some	·	·	down	· ·
so	·	·	dad	· ·
not	·	·	big	· ·
then	·	·	when	· ·
it's	·	·	just	· ·

Trace and write

see	now
looked	came
very	oh
look	about
don't	got
come	their
will	people
into	your
back	put
from	could
children	house
him	old
Mr	too
get	by

Trace and write

day		called
made		here
time		off
I'm		asked
if		saw
help		make
Mrs		an

Numbers

Trace and write

one		seven
two		eight
three		nine
four		ten
five		eleven
six		twelve

Days of the week

Trace and write

Monday

Tuesday

Wednesday

Thursday

Friday

Saturday

Sunday

red   yellow   blue   green   pink

purple   brown   orange   black   white

Trace and write

red   purple

yellow   brown

blue   orange

green   black

pink   white

Writing an invitation

Dear _____

You are invited to
my birthday party
on _____
at _____

Love from

_____